Songs of the Marketplace

NIYI OSUNDARE

SONGS OF
THE MARKETPLACE

© Niyi Osundare 1983
© Biodun Jeyifo, the Introduction

All rights reserved. No part of this publication may be reproduced or transmitted in any form or by any means without the prior written permission of the copyright holder.

ISBN 978-2266-10-8

Reissue 2006

First published 1983 by
New Horn Press Ltd, Ibadan, Nigeria

Distributed outside Africa by
African Books Collective, Oxford, UK
www.africanbookscollective.com

Michigan State University Press
www.msupress.msu.edu

Printed by Lightning Source

CONTENTS

	Page
Introduction – Biodun Jeyifo	vii
Opening	1
Poetry Is	3
Songs of Home and Around	5
Excursions	7
Sule Chase	16
'Rithmetic of Ruse	19
Siren	21
Publish or Perish	24
At a University Congregation	28
The Nigerian Railway	30
The Sand Seer	31
Ignorance	33
Udoji	35
Reflections	37
On Seeing a Benin Mask in a British Museum	39
To the Dinosaur	41
The Fall of the Beast	43
The Horseman Cometh	45
Soweto	47

Namibia Talks	49
Zimbabwe	52
For Hiroshima	55
For Bob Marley	57
Prisoners of Conscience	59
Mindscope	62
New Creed	64
Homecoming	66
Unfolding Season	71
Dry Season	73
Cloudwatch	74
The Eclipse	76
Dawn (I)	78
Dawn (II)	80
Sundown	82
Autumn (I)	83
Autumn (II)	85
Closing	87
I Sing of Change	89

INTRODUCTION

The word is out that recent, post-Civil War Nigerian literature in English has found its most comprehensive thematic expansion and remarkable technical innovations in poetry. Literary history of course cautions us to be wary of apparent truths and premature judgments. A decade and a half may be an important time secion in the experience of a generation, but it counts for little in the life of a society and the crystallization of a cultural or literary movement. Even so, there is no denying the poetic deluge in Nigerian literature at the present time. On some university campuses now, poetry readings draw almost as much enthusiastic,, appreciative audiences as do dramatic productions. And within the republic of writers, the fraternity of poets grows and bourgeons beyond those of playwrights and novelists.

This piece on Niyi Osundare then is particularly informed by this poetic deluge which some have called a poetic revolution or renaissance and which Funso Aiyejina, one of the "new" poets has, in an inspired, if collectively self promoting description, called an "alter-native tradition." Osundare occupies an increasingly looming place within this tradition. His poetry constitutes a distinct revolution within the new poetic "revolution." This observation requires some clarification before we come to an appreciation of Niyi Osundare's poetry in its own right.

Within the major genres of literature, the poetic genre has perhaps been the most problematic for our writers, given the peculiar historical and cultural factors which determined the emergence and course of development of modern African literature. It seems that within the specific genre of poetry, all the problems of a literature which arose from the womb of colonial society and is still struggling to free itself from the ambiguous legacies of its origins, achieve their most concentrated form. This is not the place to go into these problems. The essential point is that for each individual writer, and incidentally for our collective literary development, the colonial legacy and its most problematic manifestation - the umbilical ties to metropolitan European traditions - must be transcended by the forging of a distinctive voice and a demonstrable rootedness in our own realities and experience.

In the genre of poetry, more than in the genres of drama and prose fiction, these obligations and demands are more daunting for its practitioners, for the reason that while poetry seems to be the easiest, the most compact genre to "exploit," it is in fact the most "exploitative", the most "tyrannical" and rigorous of the literary genres. Thus it is that while "instant" poets are easily made, while indeed literary history is replete with legions of would be poets, the true poets belong to a disappointingly undemocratic, charmed circle of the elect of the literary firmament.

We should not of course mystify poetry and the process of poetic creation. What has been said of literature in general is truer of poetry in particular: it is 90 percent perspiration and 10 percent inspiration. In our new dispensation of post-civil war poetry, while there are constant flashes of inspiration, the perspiration is notably scanty. And the most dramatic manifestation of this situation is the relationship of the "new" poets to language and words. For while language may be the enabling medium of all literature, it is the special forte for poetry, simultaneously the bulwark and love of the true poets and the trap, the Achilles' heel, of would-be poets.

Niyi Osundare's central, looming position in the new poetry derives, first of all, from this issue of language.

It has been justifiably remarked that the "new" poetry differs from the "old," pre-Civil War poetic vintage of Okigbo, Soyinka, Echeruo and Clark, as much in the new subjects and themes of poetic expression as in the "demystification" of the language of poetry. For while the older poets generally deployed a diction and a metaphoric, highly allusive universe calculated to exclude all but a small coterie of specialists, the new poets have taken the language of poetry, the diction of figurative expression, to the market-place - to the popular daily press even. This "revolution" in the attitude to received poetic diction assumes the character of the informing aesthetic, the defining poetics of Osundare's writings.

Words and images delight and excite Osundare in the way that a painter in love with his calling delights in colours, and a sculptor who works in molten bronze enthuses in the plasticity of his medium. Thus, while most of the poets of the new "alter-native" tradition have adopted the diction of ordinary speech and the accents of popular idioms in place of the arcane latinates and the learned, allusive pedantry of much of the poetic diction of the Pre-Civil War poets, Osundare, within this "revolution" of poetic diction, has kept his metaphoric and semantic range copiously and manifoldly wide.

The most engrossing manifestation of this quality of Osundare's poetry is his sustained meditation, in poem after poem, on the nature and obligations of poetic creation and the means and logistics of its execution. The first poem of this volume, the first of his work to be published, established this ambience of Osundare's verses. Appropriately, the poem is titled "Poetry is". We can usefully quote from some of the short, condensed, epiphanic stanzas of this poetic "manifesto":

> Poetry is
> a lifespring
> which gathers timbre
> the more throats it plucks
> harbinger of action
> the more minds it stirs
>
> Poetry is
> the hawker's ditty
> the eloquence of the gong
> the lyric of the marketplace
> the luminous ray
> on the grass's morning dew
>
> Poetry is
> no oracle's kernel
> for a sole philosopher's stone
>
> Poetry
> is
> man
> meaning
> to
> man.

Within the four volumes of Osundare's poetry, the following are some of the more refreshing, illuminating variations on this sustained meditation on the process of poetic creation in particular, and the artist's vocation or calling in general: "I sing of Change", "I wake up this morning", "A Dialogue of Drums", "A Grass in the Meadow", "I Rise Now", and most of the poems in the section titled "Inflaming Flares" in the volume *A Nib in the Pond*. In the present volume, some poems like "Art for Ass Sake" and "Questions for a Pandering Poet" define the poetic vocation negatively, and with subtle irony, through satirical lampoons on what Osundare regards as the corruption of the true transformative, humanistic revolutionary ends of poetry. For if it is true that the muse of poetry has chosen him for her own, it is equally true that the dialectics of revolution have found a habitation in his poetry.

Let us neither mince words nor lay ourselves open to the charge of overstating the case here. In all modern African poetry, *all*, I repeat, only in the poetry of Agostinho Neto and David Diop will you find the same depth and passion and lyricism in solidarity with the oppressed, the downtrodden, the dispossesed, and a corresponding faith in their aspiration and will to revolutionary change as we confront in Osundare's poetry. The dispossession of the majority of our people, and more specifically of the rural producers, may in fact be said to be the grand theme of Osundare's poetry.

A descriptive, paraphrasing criticism will characterise such a passionate solidarity with the dispossessed as we get in Osundare's poetry as "Poetry of engagement or commitment". But this is now an outworn label in contemporary African literary criticism. We need a different order of critical discourse and a different conceptual framework to grasp this phenomenon. I propose a modified form of Hegelian dialectics: if it is true that certain writers seek to express the most basic truths of an age in their art, it is equally true that the period itself "chooses" certain writers as the vehicles for the expression of these truths. Only such a dialectical interplay of the subjective, personal choice of the poet, and the objective, relentless impingement of realities and forces which refuse to be ignored, which demand resolution for historical advance to take place, only such an interplay will explain how the poetry of Diop and

Neto, and now Osundare, can so totally and passionately encompass the aspirations of Africa's disposessed masses and their will to revolutionary change. Is it any wonder that only in the works of these three poets, in the entire corpus of modern African poetry, do we confront just as much immersion in the realities and multifarious lineaments of Africa's underdevelopment as an internationalist dimension of solidarity with all the world's oppressed peoples.

You will thus read in Osundare's volumes sometimes humorous, often searing, occasionally bitter and satirical, but always vivid and metaphorically arresting evocations of episodes from our recent history and the upheavals, triumphs and defeats of struggles in Nigeria and other lands. You will encounter celebrations of defenders of the oppressed and the scourge and terror of the oppressors. Above everything else, the justification of the will to revolution in Osundare's poetry is based on a vigorous, sustained solicitate for one of the world's oldest producers: the peasants, those who till the soil, and their quasi-mystical ties to the earth.

The land, the people and the natural rhythms and cycles are given poignant but unsentimental evocation. The kind of sensibility which informs Mao's and Neto's poetry on the land and the people comes to mind, the difference being that Osundare would have nothing of the austere rigour of these poets; for him it is all metaphoric exuberance. This strain is dominant in the second part of the present volume titled "Songs of Dawn and Seasons". Here, even in a love poem, "Unfolding Seasons", the poet's observant, sensitive eye on nature yields the insight that the processes of the natural world correspond to the wishes and yearnings of the heart and, by extension, the will to change, the will to freedom. Contrastively, evocations of seasons of natural dryness and blight on the land, in other poems, lead the poet to muse on the "unnatural" deserts and scarcities created by man.

What Osundare's poetry seems to me to demonstrate then, is the truth that the immediacy and power of revolutionary poetry, *mature* revolutionary poetry, derive from a frank, perhaps even unapologetic importunateness. The revolutionary poet, hardly ever content to adopt the tactics of impersonality or self-effacement, everywhere secretes his self, his opinions and perceptions into his poetry. The expected consequence of this is, of course, that the exemplary "self" proferred or the opinions and perceptions advanced will jolt complacent sensibilities out of their placid state, rouse the appropriate social classes and strata to awareness and action or productively agitate that dialectical space between accommodation and resistance in a given social order. Within this *constant*, there is however the important qualification that intrusive secretion of self, opinions and perceptions in the poetry, deploys varied tactics and wears many masks and disguises, some more or less adequate or effective than others.

The "voices" and "songs" highlighted in Osundare's titles relate precisely to this factor finding the personae, the media and idioms to carry the burden of his idealistic, utopian projections beyond the contradictions and negations of the present Nigerian, and by extension and implication, African social order. Thus, it is a veritable losing, though enormously invigorating, battle to keep track of the myriad tactics and masks of expressing revolutionary views adopted by this poet. If the "message" of Osundare's poetry is so strongly embedded in metaphor and imagery, proverbs and aphorisms, this is the more effective in the context of the accessible, lucid poetic he uses. For it is probable that in due course Osundare will attract attention or achieve recognition as much for his meticulous, consumate deftness in the craft, the technique, the logistics of poetic expression as for his radical utopian views. For me at any rate, his greatest promise now is that these two aspects of literary expression are fused in his poetry, and this again marks another point of departure from much of the earlier Nigerian English-Language poetry, where style and technique are so displaced from the substance or content of poetic expression that they often draw attention to themselves as the end of literary expression. Osundare is, again, in the company of Neto here, where crafts is neither superior to, nor subservient to substance or content. And like Neto, the range of his technical and stylistic options are quite impressive, stretching from the part transliterated, part adapted re-working of traditional formal verbal rhetoric and songs to the austere, terse, sculptural relief of poems like "The Nigerian Railway", "Mindscope", "New Creed", and the arresting poetic pictogram, Sundown".

I do not want to give the impression of perfection, of a definitive arrival in the poetic trajectory of Niyi Osundare. Definitely, the "errors of rendering" (Okigbo's wry self-criticism) are all there. But I do think that Funso Aiyejina's cautionary observation that Osundare's heavy but exultantly flexible use of oral resources may "become a mere echo of a familiar form, that of the oral tradition", if Osundare does not "hew a distinct personal poetic style". — I do believe that this observation is insuportable from the evidence of even this first volume. Osundare's is the most distinctive voice among our new poets; and I would like to suggest that this may be explained by the fact that in his verses, we confront both poetry of revolution and a revolution in poetry, in terms of forms and techniques.

Censorious critics may plausibly charge Osundare with technical, logistical fastidiousness. An obvious illustration of this would be the deliberate symmetry in the arrangement of the poems and sections of each of his volumes to correspond suggestively with seasonal and calendrical cycles, and in the case of this volume with sunrise and sunset. However, inspite of, or coincident with this logistical fastidiousness, Osundare's poetry beathes and pulses with life and vitality. In his poetry abstractions like poverty, exploitation, corruption and dependence assume concrete, searing vividness.

His lines reveal a lucid, witty lyricism, sharply etched imagery, earthy, often deliberately raucous turns of phrase, closeness to the people, to the earth, closeness to nature. A major analysis could indeed be offered of Osundare's handling of *nature* in a way that is perhaps unique in contemporary Nigerian literature, oscillating as it does, between the accustomed animist ritualism of older poets like Okigbo and Soyinka, and careful sensitive observation and description, with something of a naturalist's eye, and the moral-philosophical rubric of projecting the processes of nature as a model and a paradigm for change and renewal in society.

Like music, like religion, poetry often serves to cushion the poet and his audience against the negations of an unjust, exploitative and alienating social order as things to be endured, accommodated and ultimately sublimated. Revolutionary poetry however problematises both these negations and the very accommodation to them which non-revolutionary poetry insinuates. The lyrical and metaphorical exuberance and vision of Osundare does exactly this in its expression of revolutionary poetry in Nigeria.

Biodun Jeyifo,
University of Ife

> *I made an unbreakable pledge to myself*
> *That the people would find their voices in my*
> *song.*
>
>   Pablo Neruda

opening . . . . .

Poetry is

not the esoteric whisper
of an excluding tongue
not a claptrap
for a wondering audience
not a learned quiz
entombed in Grecoroman lore

Poetry is
a lifespring
which gathers timbre
the more throats it plucks
harbinger of action
the more minds it stirs

Poetry is
the hawker's ditty
the eloquence of the gong
the lyric of the marketplace
the luminous ray
on the grass's morning dew

Poetry is
what the soft wind
musics to the dancing leaf

what the sole tells the dusty path
what the bee hums to the alluring nectar
what rainfall croons to the lowering eaves

Poetry is
no oracle's kernel
for a sole philosopher's stone

Poetry
is
man
meaning
to
man.

songs
 of
  home
   and
    around

Excursions

I

We meet eyes in sunken sockets
teeth bereft of gum
skins scaly like iguana's
feet swollen like watermelon

We meet babies with chronic hydrocephalus
squeezing spongy breasts
on mother's bony chests,
shrivelled

We see village boys' kwashiorkor bellies
hairless heads impaled on pin necks
and ribs baring the benevolence
of the body politic

the family head roams the bush
trapping rats and insects
and cocoa bags in prosperous wait
for the trip to liverpool

in city fringes pregnant women
rummage garbage heaps for
the rotting remnants of city tables
above, hawks and vultures hovering
for their turn

We see the farmer shaving earth's head
with a tiny hoe, his back a creaking
bow of disintegrating discs
from dawn's dew to dusk's dust
offering futile sacrifices
to a creamless soil

halfnude, toughbiceped labourers
troop in tipperfuls from sweatfields
drilled by foremen soulless like
a slavemaster, a few kobo greet
the miserly homecoming
of a pilgrimage of misery

at the Local Govt. Lottery
the crowd snakes across the alley
it is Friday
and time to brawl and dream

on street pavements women delouse
each other in busy reciprocity
nits, defiant like palm kernels,
explode between the nails

rats and roaches compete
in the inner room
and lizards play
hide-and-seek in wall cracks

in the neighbourhood church
the faithful sing into
catatonic orgasms,
hymning and psalming are the diet
of the soul though the body succumbs
to the buffets of hunger
between belches the plump preacher
extols the virtue of want,
the only ticket to the wealth beyond

several government people
have passed through these streets
several Mercedes tyres have drenched
gaunt road liners in sewer water
several sanitary inspectors have come
in formidable helmets and gas masks
but rot and *tanwiji** escape
the uniformed eye

poverty is an invisible thing

---

*mosquito larvae.

II)

Beggars line our route
running sores of broken humanity
they line our route
crippling metaphors of our disabled conscience

Some living casualties of our recent war
  the war we fought
  to make politicians rich
  and the country poor
  Some victims of a raging war
  across the borders
  battered grass in the battle
  of mindless elephants
  they display angular babies
  extracting sympathy pennies
  from passers-by

Some crawl like crabs
neither seeing nor hearing
unsettling issues of malnourished pregnancies

Many have limbs and eyes and ears
only beggared by unceasing layoffs,
handy jettisons of captains of industry.

Paltry pennies rattling begging bowls
is music to the ears of God

charity echoes over
the nagging whisper
of a long and stubborn guilt

These sightless sockets
burn indictory gazes into
heavy pockets
and vaults of hoarded loot
these swinging stumps
are pointers to
the skull behind our corpulent grins

III)

I have been through
the push and pull
of shopping doors
queueing before
red-lipped damsels
fingering cash registers
insolent like a January harmattan

I have been through
the jam and jab
of motor-parks
molue, danfo, dagbere*
and ear-slaying horns
harsher than Hitler's siren
porters and omolanke**
crumble under smuggled merchandise

---
*names of passenger vehicles
**hand-pushed cart

and touts strain for a pluck
at the hawking girls' oranges
the just-come county trader
dissolves in tears
as pick-purses brawl
over the loot
across the street

"Ikere Ogoga!" Ado Ewi!" "Efon Alaaye!"
The *agbero's** itenerant throat
explodes a route-lined chaos
on frightful passengers.
His brass ring has circled death
off the road

I have been through
the secretariat
where civil servants
are all but civil
here files are
lost and found
found and lost
by mysterious messengers' magic

The correspondence tray
is the coffin of ailing democracy
Pending
is heavier than
Out

---
*tout

12

and both together are leaner than
IN
The precarious tilt on the master's bureau
engenders a rift outside the doors
the tremours are felt
to the roots of the house.

IV

In the streets
people whisper their rage
about a million million
naira of our blood
multiplying foreign fortunes
and the damnable years
of our blind slavery.

In University corridors
students talk
about theadbare gurus
recycling worn traditions
dreading change like despots
yes, they talk about dons
pawning wives for chairs
then slouching into glamorized mediocrity
breeding flat minds
diplomaed with the slavish stamp
of received gospels

In the village
people talk
about the old confusing age with wit

making grey hair excuse
for frosted folly
demanding a world prostrate
like a fossilized lizard salaaming
to the stiff orders
of hoary tyranny

In the cities
people whisper
about fortressed kings
ruling by boot and butt,
sirens kniving through
the turbid squalor
of slums like the butcher's saw
dancing through the abdomen
of a coughing cow
they put a price on wit
stocking dissident throats
with bullets from foreign friends
Rabid amnesiacs,
history slips through their claws,
galloping Jehus who see nothing in
the rear mirror of time.

In the markets
people talk
about bloated millionaires
hostaging us to slave makers:
exporters
importers
emergency contractors

manufacturers' representatives
buying cheap
selling dear
whoring through gory deals
to Mammon's throne
bartering conscience
for a chip of greedy glitter

But soon
the people will shout
when murmurs break through muzzles
and will powers into action
then oppression's cloud will clear
the sun eastering hence
a life full and free.

Sule Chase

The chase starts in some shadowy stall
On a hungry afternoon
"Oleee barawoooooo onye oshiiiii"
Rises from tepid earth
To the baking skies

A barrel-buttocked woman blows the whistle
For the fastest race in Lagos
Since the awesome B26 nudged
A slumbrous city into chaos
Forcing brothels in every street
To cough out their putrefying entrails

* * * * * * * * * * *

The race gathers more legs
In every lane
Tailors with giant scissors
Permsecs with PENDING files
Barristers with dusty wigs
NEPA* experts with fused bulbs
Telephonists in dead head-sets
The doctor with a coughing stethoscope
The don with his chair aloft
The sergeant just gone to inspect

*Nigerian Electricity Power Authority

His tenth mansion (you can never trust
Contractors: they've grown so smart
Since the first batallion of oil rigs
Besieged our shores)
The housemaid with the W.C. broom
Reuter agents dying not to miss
The show (its cinematographic
Recreation is fortune across the shores)
All skinning each other's heels
Surging for the virgin blow

And Sule has
The onceinalife luck
Of leading Lagos in a race

*   *   *   *   *   *   *   *   *

Sule climbs mountains
Of fresh assorted garbage
Traverses valleys
Of liquefied stench
Tears through traffic
In bumpertobumper grave
And loops into an alley,
Target of brute missiles
From every corner

And then Sule feels his strength
Buckle for the first time

His forehead oozes some blood
(Not enough to go round)
His head hollows into swirls
A thousand stars besiege his eyes
And his legs turn into *ekan**
Snapping at the first harmattan winds
He falls, insensate to a prick.

The crowd swarm on Sule,
Soldier ants on a speck
In the leopard's trail
The tailor stabs him
With his scissors
NEPA with his bulb
The doctor with his stethoscope
The sergeant with his belt
(He lost his gun in the chase)
The housemaid with her broom
The don with a well enunciated
Epithet from the OED**
The lawyer, adjusting his bib,
Condemns Sule for autoliquidation

* * * * * * * * * *

Hours Later
The Homicide Unit arrives
For an onthespot arrest
They arrest Sule's corpse
His left hand clutching
A rumpled three **kobo loal**

---

*elephant grass
**Oxford English Dictionary

'Rithmetic of Ruse

(Reflections 79)

We murder truth
and burn sophistical candles
in search of illusion
A calculated cloud is let down
by satanic computers coughing
cataclysms in algebraic quantum.

Theirs is the 'rithmetic of deceit
powers hunters wallowing through wiles
to a minus throne
cooking numbers for a gullible mass

They have fractioned
a fragmented whole
and the splinters will smother
them in their thousands
men born with long crowns
have miscounted those
they claim to rule
the cows enfranchised by them
will freely impale them
on their wavering horns
leaving us with our search
for the fragments of truth.

Power prostitutes now going
to labour will deliver
a townful of monsters to jolt
our anaesthesia of conscience
before they put fangs
in our lying throats.

Siren

(Music of the Visiting Power)

Siren Siren Siren
Police acrobats on motorbikes
wielding whips with consummate despatch
the road must be cleared at once
for which worthy ruler
ever shares the right of way?

Siren Siren Siren
the clangorous convoy
of powers and power brokers
conditioned in Mercedes back
far, very far, from the maddening crowd

Siren Siren Siren
kwashiorkored children
waving tattered flags
in the baking sun
(they forfeited the day's meal
to cheer their Excellencies)
orchestrated cultural dancers
dripping drums of sweat
in rafia shrouds
partymen kangarooing
to keep the crowd in place

Siren Siren Siren
Even on highways where potholes
snail the jaguar
they manage not to see
a land debowelled by erosion
cornfields withering
and yam tendrils yellowing
on tubers smaller than a palm kernel
blind are they
to the seeds of tomorrow's famine

Siren Siren Siren
and buntings and banners
and brazen bombasts
their Excellencies love
the sound of words

Siren Siren Siren
no time for dry days
and dark nights
or food whose price
costs a ton of gold
no time for hospitals
and schools and roads
their Excellencies are not here
for the begging bickerings
of a faceless rural crowd

Sirren siren siren
and the air heavy
with love of state

organized grins
made up cheers
rehearsed pledges

But babies contorted
in mothers' backs
are question marks
for tomorrow's answer.

Publish or Perish

(for Professor Ajijepepa)

Tell me
Do you think they will accept this,,
The A & P,*
Do you think they will?

Just see
There are only a dozen references
Footnotes don't wind across pages
The bibliography says nothing about
Plato and Thucyidides
Aristotle and Pythagoras

The language, watery
No "ab initio", "ceteris paribus"
"Horribile dictu", "mutatis mutandi"
To think of a learned paper
In this unattic idiom

And the home smell of the journal
Not referred in New York
Printed in Yokohama
Published in Londnn

---

*Appointments and Promotions (Committee), the Nigerian University's erratic Inquisition

Frozen with the imprimatur
Of an Oxonian emeritus
Not disputationed on
Chaucer or Shakespeare
But written
On Soyinka or Amadi

This paper chase
Is our swiftest contribution
To knowledge
Hallmark of true scholarship
Fastest mark of progress

Grovel before the editor
And dust his shoes
Don't miss his birthday
And his daughter's too
Pawn your wife for a promissory note
Acceptance letters are legal tender
On our promotion market

Papers papers papers
Let them come
In sheaves and bales
In trailers and lorries
In trucks and wheelbarrows
Syndicated, duplicated
Pirated, plagiarized
Suffice that they will be foreign
and arcane enough

To strengthen our claim
To erudite universality

The typist may stumble
Stencils may run short
NEPA's epilepsy may last a month
While offices roast their tenants
Like berbecued hogs
Laboratory chemicals may run dry
And equipment antediluvian
The bookstore may go empty
As the library turns archive
In dated acquisition
Teaching load may hunch
Your horse's back
But churn them out in dizzying quantum
How else is a true genius known
But by making paper bricks
Without straw

Papers papers papers
Pillar of our cardboard tower
Scaffold of our building nation
Pulp test of our collective wisdom

You can tell a house by its door
A person by his dress

A university by its papers
In our papyrus soar into archaidemia
It is papers, papers, papers
Or nothing

At a University Con-Gre-Gation

After all this
do your still ask
why our feet are stuck
in yesterday's mud
and every step
is a waddle and a trip?

Jargons take over the podium
and slogans rumble
in the belly of the hall
fustian grenades detonate
and eggheads explode
with barren approbation

In this desert only
grow the harlequinade
or ritual
and the apotheosis
of custom
fearful of change
like a sterile despot

Narrow minds wide follies
spectacled eyes
afraid of veering beyond the nose

O my people
you stray
seeking here
a way across the wilderness

The Nigerian Railway

dark sna
ky str
uctures
 tor tuous
milli
 pede on
legs
 of iron
crawl ing
wear ily

fromswamptosavannah.

The Sand Seer

Let your wandering fingers
Trek in these sands
And open up the vista
To the mystery of time

You cast no nuts
Fling no cords
Ring no bells
Nor seek yesterlives
At the root of graveyard turf.

Vista atoms of practised
Eyes, seen everywhere
Knowing the secret of
Every toe. Truths lie
Undressed and the riddle
Of the morrow is cracked
Upon a grain of sooth.

Let the sparkle of these
Sands telescope enigmatic
Time and catch the bird on
Tomorrow's tree.

which woman makes best wife
which profession makes richest
men, what to do or undo that
I may live till I please?

The future shrinks to eye-shot
As you sit there counting
Lots in grains of sand.

Ignorance

The cow is dying
for a trip to London
let it go
it will come back
as corned beef

Ignorance
Kinsvice of superstition
tyranny's nurture
and wills
cowing instead of kicking

Hitler armed ignorance
to fight the world
won the first battle
against reason
and enthroned the superstition
of Aryan superiority

At last
the pogrom
and a world ablaze

Madaru steals public funds
and blocks the road
with a sleek Mercedes
custommade from Germany
they sing his praises
and envy his luck

Madaru buys a crown
and becomes a king

And you ask:
how could sheep all agree
to give their crown to a wolf?

Ignorance
father of unknowing
what every master
wants in his servant
what every *baas*
wants in his nigger.

Udoji*

the stepmother afraid
of being thought wicked
feeds her stepson
till he constipates
the braggart accused
of shrunken arms
kills forty lame
to prove his valiance

We ask for food and water
to keep our toiling frames
on the hoe
but they innundate us with udoji

now pockets burst with arrears
but market stalls are empty
gari is dearer than eyes
a naira cannot buy a yam

when a bribe is too heavy
it impoverishes the giver

---

*In 1975, following the release of a Salary Review Panel headed by Chief Jerome Udoji, government workers and some in the private sector received inflationary salaries and arrears. Chief Udoji's name became a metaphor for his bonanza.

tell the givers of this bribe
that what we need
is more than money can buy

Reflections

There are a thousand spectacles
At the forge of the uncircumcised
There is a heap of words
In a penny newspaper

The *babalawo* charms off the clouds
But marvels at a scorched land
The lizard feeds on its own brood
And wonders why they say it buries
Its future in its guts;

Ayederu empties the government treasury
For a generous donation to a
Church Building Foundation
He receives special prayers
And commandership of the
Order of Saint Michael

"We are all equal before the Lord'
Says the pious clergy in cassock
And collar, "Jews and Gentiles,
Peter and Judas, Boers and Kaffirs,
Nixon and Allende"

We are all equal:
Cocoacoffectea growers pushing
Bellies bloated by kwashiorkor
And cocoacoffeetea drinkers
Fighting a losing battle with overnourishment

The world is like Solel Boneh's steam-shovel
It scoops earth from one place
To fill up the hole in another.

On Seeing A Benin Mask In A British Museum

(for FESTAC 77)

Here stilted on plastic
A god deshrined
Uprooted from your past
Distanced from your present
Profaned sojourner in a strange land

Rescued from a smouldering shrine
By a victorianizing expedition
Traded in for an O.B.E.
Across the shores

Here you stand, chilly,
Away from your clothes
Gazed at by curious tourists savouring
Parallel lines on your forehead
Parabola on your cheek
Semicircles of your eye brows
And the solid geometry of your lips
Here you stand
Dissected by alien eyes.

Only what becomes is becoming
A noose does not become a chicken's neck
Who ever saw a deity dancing *langbalangba**
To the carious laugh of philistine revellers?

> *Iya jajeji l'Egbe*
> *Ile eni l'eso ye'ni***

Retain the tight dignity of those lips
Unspoken grief becomes a god
When all around are alien ears
Unable to crack the kernel of the riddle.

---

*langbalangba: undignifingly; gracelessly
**Suffering afflicts the stranger in an alien land
  One is most valued in one's own home.

To the Dinosaur

Now the gale has blown
The secret of the chicken's arse is known

There are uncountable feet
In this world of races
Yours were shaped facing backwards
And so you have picked up the horsetail
And danced through blood into prehistory

If we don't know
Where we are going
At least we know
Where we are coming from;
Knowing neither,
You have torn down the gate
And asked wolves to tend your sheep.

A hollow head craving
The weight of a crown
A doddering hand swapping
Daggers for a sceptre
You have sold out two million
Skeletons to purchase a gilded skull.

The owl perches on the *iroko*
And hoots out a tune:
The whip that carved weals
On the first wife
Will descend from the rafter someday
To give the new bride a stroke of history
After Notre Dame
Came Waterloo
And then St. Helena.

Then you will surely fade into prehistory
Remembered only when tales are told
Of midday dreams
And spectres on the market day.

The Fall of the Beast

(for the Sandinistas)

The hyena falls
In the jungle
Its blustering whiskers
Matted with venom

Bazookaed is the heart
Of odium and flint
Muted the mouth
That decreed a million deaths

The beast slumps
Its grabbing fingers
Stiff like its statue's
Unclawed the loot
Of Nicaragua's blood

Bulleted the fang
Bathed in blood and bile
Brained the hulk
Of repressing dynasties
Bolstered by baser beasts abroad

Drums and horns in Managua
Celebrant, of the end of torture

Another lesson
In a forest
That never learns.

The Horseman Cometh

A horseman gallops to power
and tyrants of all the world rejoice
torture chambers multiply apace
and the noose thickens, descending

A real horseman for sure
(not the old makebelieve)
with promises of a heroic past
when white was white
and black was black
and the rich ruled
the world by right

A new horseman
with guns in the saddle
one for dissidents at home
another for maddening rivals
in the land of the rising sun

A new horseman
with trust in might
he will build arsenals
in place of barns
and prod the poor
to gorge on bullets

But the grass shall rise
bladed against pounding hoofs
a new gust of will
shall tell the hoary equestrian
that the turf indeed has changed

Soweto

Youthfire burns out
the accumulated lethargy of many years

Today is asking questions
that burned yesterday
in the mouth

A kaffired will
other-check turning
till a jaw of anguish
agitated a tongue of revolt:

it must end, this slave life must end
heloted squattered squalored kraaled
booted butted robbened hanged carcassed

plundered of sweat
fleeced for the robement
of colder climes
by monster merchants
of the skin

First
>   SHARPVILLE
Now
>   SOWETO

These murdered flowers
blossoming
will fruit in freedom
These rising shoots
will tree into free spaces
beyond tomorrow.

Namibia Talks

"South Africa Police
murders seven hundred Blacks in Soweto '

    "The U.N. condemns the action".

"South Africa occupies Southern Angola
murdering women and children
burning barns and farms"

    "The U.N. partly condemns the action"

"South Africa postpones Namibia
independence by a hundred years"
(she will keep by force
the land she got by ruse)

    "The OAU craves sanctions
    prays the Western Con-Tact Group
    to do their job"

Blind four hundred years
just when shall we see
the corroding conspiracy
of life takers?

Multiple victims of double talk
when end this deafening dialogue
with the shifty jaws of death?

For so long have we mistrusted our sheep
to the care of leopards
we have woken to the whitened skeleton
of talkative folly

Now seek we freedom
in the hand of habitual slavers
How dare we seek life
From those who profit
by death?

Blacksmiths, assemble
assemble
from the Limpopo to the Volta
forge anew the armoury
of will and action
Time to stop shooting words
at those who dialogue
with rockets and mortars

We shall turn our eyes
from the setting sun
whose dying flickers
entomb our vision

with our own hands
we shall take our life
from the coffin of death merchants

America
will always
veto
and Britain
　abstain

Zimbabwe

for Josiah Tongogara
for every guerilla who fought the war
that turned Rhodesia into Zimbabwe

The cock has crowed
ushering in a free dawn

Iroko has sprouted
in a lot begrudged
to elephant grass.

Here we are
after ship wrecked talks
and jungles of blood
after countless treacheries
by men collared out of our fold
by the folly of ghostly power

The cock has crowed

Here the end
of those who pillage
others' huts
to mend their own

the end
of those
who build liberty statues
on a pillar of torture

The cock has crowed

Not in vain
have guns boomed
Not in vain
are children orphans
Not in vain
are wives widows
before they are
five and twenty

The cock has crowed

Those who vowed
there will be no freedom
in their lifetime
encountered freedom
in the graveyard of their dream

Yet another milepost
on the sizzling roads
from Cairo to Cape

The cock has crowed

The ruins have risen
every chip and every grain,
a liberating stone
in the monument
of our struggle.

The cock has crowed
ushering in a free dawn

Iroko has sprouted
in a lot begrudged
to elephant grass.

For Hiroshima

when reason goes up
in flames (power) lust
gathers the ashes

it has always been
the survival of the brutest

when bloodmen send fireatoms
on massacre missions
a legion unaware of the powerwrestle
are guineapigs in a tinderbox

earth and sky in
clouds of dismemberments
cascades of roasting humans

they who perish
may count for those
in love with numbers
but they may never enter the books

whom savage fire consumes
by instalment

at Hiroshima
the casualties
never die

For Bob Marley

The songbird has fallen
in the forest of wails
Leaves throb
in the elegy of the wind

You assail the horror of the slum
exploding its raw rhythms
in the indifferent ears
of a deafening world

You ask them to
Get up, Stand up
whom oppression crouches
like lethal lumbago
and squatters smell the open secret
of the dunghill

Ah! the songbird has fallen

You who put positive vibration
in the stunned heart
of a deadening lull
consciences were dormant
till you stirred them up

You shot the sheriff
with a chord of protest
and scorned rat race
in the mad alleys
of concrete jungles

Alas, Zion's Train has stopped
a distant shout from the home station

Let them weep
their crocodile tears
in Montego Bay
who chased you
through wood and grass
but now die to frame you up
in mute marble

Let them sheathe their chisel
who now want to arrest in stone
the locks they dreaded

For you are star
of a softer planet

The songbird has fallen
in the forest of wails
Leaves throb
in the elegy of the wind

Prisoners of Conscience

(for Ngugi wa Thiong 'o)

Another mind is cast against
Bare walls of fortified mindslaughter
By gagsmiths with steel muzzles
On the mouth of conscience

Truth dazzles their eyes
Like sunrays of a tropical midday
Burns their throats
Like a witch's hot iron
Scared of dawn's return
They seek to clog the throat
That foresings the daysong

Encysted in turreted palaces
They foment universal silence
Dreading voices above the hush
In palaces they feast, the din
Of clinking glasses submerging
The swansong of children
On mothers' laps contorted
Like question marks
In palaces they feast
In the colony of foreign vultures

Bald neck up with wiles of plunder
In palaces they loot,
Yesterday's freedom warriors
Now cage builders,
Erectors of torture chambers

But the day must break
So the people can see
For seeing is knowing
Knowing is telling
Sawdust from *gari*[1]
Knowing is ending evil
With those who endow evil with
A portfolio in statesmanship

So the sun harried west
By habitual plunderers
Shall emerge from the east
It shall emerge
With powerrays in every nook
Radiating the shadowy brood
of hush owls

All shall be radiant
Like the morning
On creation day
Every throat shall
Have a song
Every song
An ear

---

1 Grainy cassava flour, a staple food in West Africa.

The truth shall come
Straightening out itself
After twisted journeys
Across the earth

Then ears shall believe
What mouths say
Hosts shall throw doors
Open to strangers at night

Then blinkers shall fall
So the people can see
They shall see truth
Tearing through the clouds
Undulating beachwards with the waves
Springing from the earth
Like pure waterhead
Rustling through the leaves
Like a brisksteady morning breeze

All clear
They shall see the men who mule
Those they vowed to rule.

Mindscope

    (for B.J.)

"Thou shalt not", they say
"Why not?!", I ask

and instantly turning
an eddy of questions
my mind probes belief's underbelly
pulps tradition's iron curtain
into paper screen unriddled
with the nib of search

WHY
unevils a cyclorama of seeing
deep expanse of knowing
across a radiant universe of vision

mindscoping truths contrabanded
by dogma, embargoed by mystery's
customs, uniformed guards of nescience

and rays fall back
enlightening doubts,
radiating marvels,
levelling mountains.

to each eye, light
to each mind, question
to each conscience, will
to each will, action.

New Creed

they wrap their myths
in holy sheets
and scribble them
on the sacredest corner
of our soul

our fingers crave
foreign bubbles
scorning fatally
the substance of our home

pale gods taint
the green petals
of our opening bud
there is a greying
in the pistil of our being

now
trees lose their heads
to locusts of dogma
our confidence falls green
from pests of surrender

we will cultivate the field of faith
and replant the seeds of trust
we will till all fallow minds
and seed the earth
with a new creed.

Homecoming

(for femi, nicole)

We arrive as the sun
begins to straighten out the shadows
We arrive when east and west
are equidistant from the eye
of our sky.

The land regains all the marks
lost to sunset
We see all paths as streams
begin to change their course

Mountains level up with valleys
the horizon extends beyond the eyes
rays informs the forest
and trees sing to one another

No severing vaults can swallow
our voices, no boomerang
can agitate our throats

Let all prostrating lizards
stand
let all lions

abate their terror
Tell all pounding elephants
a trodden forest sprouts nothing
but twigs of famine
Tell the greedy fowl
to stop guzzling the eggs
of its own brood.

Let fence builders
break their hammer
Let their hand suffer
arthritic arrest
who mean to stir hornets
on a peaceful world

songs
　of
　　dawn
　　　and
　　　　seasons

Unfolding Season

You will be my *egigun**
draping forest head in silk
from the wardrobe of the season

When the harmattan doctors wounds
and winds husband pollens
for the barns of the reap season
when the sun's ripening rays
drip harvest touch
and opening pods hasten
the labour of dispersing seeds

You will be there
when through balding trees
I read time's portrait
through the sieving leaves
thickening shadows when the sun throbs
the sky's heart
and the lengthening when
it slants to a corner of its chest

You will see squirrels
rattling fallen leaves
with perforated kernels
and grasshoppers dieting
on scanty green

---
*silk cotton tree

You will see
the smoke of burning bush
and hear the faint swansong
of exploding stalks
antelopes and grasscutters
scuttling out of the flames
into the barbed welcome
of waiting arrows
Eusa,* uncaved, walking
through fire
and daylight's taboo
hawks and kites riding flame crests
for fire spoils

You will then
smell the moisture of brooks
refrigerated by leafshade
crab patterns in the sand
and watch weaverbird nests
swinging in the wind

We shall lie locked
in the pod
of an unfolding season.

---

*primordial name for Okete, a nocturnal
 rodent

Dry Seasons

The sun stands smothered
heavy clouds exchange
groans of parturition

It's a long time now
since we heard the
pattering cry ora new born:
Earth awaits in
pain of the embrace of
shafts of birth

For some time
it's been dry suffering
maize leaves toughening
into sisal, the tendril
collapsing on stakes,
heads turning dust-brown
and the earth hot like
molten steel.

> the cob this year
> will rust grey-tasseled
> the tuber undersized.

But the village knows the man
who fans the clouds away.

Cloudwatch

the shepherd is out in the field
weathered like his staff
and sparse kaftan
alone, holding a dry dialogue
with the sky

sand storms come and go
but the sky declines to spit

the sheep are all angles now
sapped on grassless miles
each cracked oasis belying
the seeming greenness of date palms

the market will pass them over
these skeletons in hairless membranes
shunned they will be
by buyers who want the   meat
and not the bone

last year the rain didn't go
on a journey
the sky had its due

and courier shafts drenched
earthbed in green
water furrowed through
myriad shoots of lush

the shepherd out in the field
watches the sun reddening palm tops
tomorrow it will rise again
at the other end of the sky
will it come a red ball
peeping through a blanket of clouds?

The Eclipse

you shouldn't have come today
no, you shouldn't have
when all eyes are up for the sun

we've just brought out
our blankets and mats
the farmer spreading out his cocoa beans
this is fermentation day
and produce buyers are waiting

you shouldn't have come today
with a dark film across the sky
we are innocent folks
we've never seen the rain wash out
the haze of december
or the sun trespass
the serenity of night

this scuffle of sun and moon
makes us wonder about boundary disputes
in heaven where we thought surveyors
were just

you shouldn't have come today
we do not want to sleep at noon
we are playful people,
serious about pleasure
we do not want the drummer to leave
when just sharpening our legs
we do not want the keg to crouch
when eyes are just turning red

Dawn (I)

fresh
    like godwine
    descending from palmtop
    at day beginning
    here strong I stand untouched
    by the water of a woken day.

soothing
    like blended serenade
    of bird and insect I
    wait open armed to embrace
    afemoju* punctual spirit
    hospitable like beach breezes
    unmasking mini dressed Yemoja
    foretreading wavewashed sands
    before acolytes' assorted toes
    trooping in for a dip

crisp
    like a flower furled
    I feel the secreting
    of early juice in
    the pistil of my knowing

---
*dawn

cool-wet like the lip of
earth this primeval hour
of my folded budding I every
essence of me am a petal
of earth's preblossoming.

Dawn (II)

Come with me at dawn
tryst time
and hear how the wasp
turned thread
in the midriff

Sit at this threshold
day's interpreter
and with lips chaste
tell why moths tease
flames with wing
gossamer than air

Dawn, sage of day
when earth closes
all books but its own
the breeze dewlined
rolls leaves into
scrolls of *Isoye**

Inchoate hour
soothtime
for straightening the twisted word
for the ears of a waking day

---
*memory aid

Dawn
is time to
recall the future
foretell the past.

Sundown

rooster roosting   hearth sizzling   sun exiting
nightbirds cooing   embers greying   orange valedicting

horizon closing   coquettes kis-   oilflames dancing
earthysky mating   sing   worms glowing
                          courters cro-
                          oning

stars winking   managers wining   elders remembering
moon beaming   labourers pining   children romping

muezzin blasting   ikoyi glowing   clubs booming
ramadan evening   ajegunle smogg-   churches brooding
                          ing

Autumn (I)

Cascades of
yellowing leaves caress
my crown; my feet
cherish the rustle.

Trees baring by
the top leak shards
of sunlight down the
roots, june's heated
wig is receding longing
for april's quick transplant

I soft-tread a carpet
of gold seeking
just seeking a bark
to clutch, each carries
nature's thorns or
thorns of parliament.

I look through
the window of falling
leaves the westering
sun begrudges feeble
rays like a swansong.

Nearby I drink
the sound of tunneling
stream tumbling into
a weir. my ear lost
midfall fishes foam
and pebble.

Home, sojourner
home now, with
squirrels starting
at your every step.

Autumn (II)

Fresh beheaded wheat
dripping sap
combine guillotines
humming triumph

Grain and chaff
tumbling into sacs
chaff and grain
winnowing day is separation day

Plummy aroma
of striated gardens
or is the aroma
all plum?

Globular tomatoes, obese,
surrender on ridge brows
juice-soft
they await the basket
and the thud of
lengthening shadows

Squelching steamlets
through the delta of the palm

Lipteasing
the apple rocks
in the hammock of the wind
twig-crashing at
ripening hour
to keep the tryst with earth

Close fisted cabbage
coy
conceals core
in foliage of crisp
hell-sweet below
a plucked umbilicus
a leafy onion of surprise
green is ripe
and the sickle
saver or ripper?

closing ....

I sing of Change

Sing on: Somewhere, at some new moon,
We'll learn that sleeping is not death,
Hearing the whole earth change its tune.

                      W.B. Yeats.

I sing
of the beauty of Athens
without its slaves

Of a world free
of kings and queens
and other remnants
of an arbitrary past

Of earth
with no
sharp north
or deep south
without blind curtains
or iron walls

of the end
of warlords and armouries
and prisons of hate and fear

Of deserts treeing
and fruiting
after the quickening rains

Of the sun
radiating ignorance
and stars informing
nights of unknowing

I sing of a world reshaped

CPSIA information can be obtained
at www.ICGtesting.com
Printed in the USA
LVHW011148260622
722140LV00003B/417